Warrior

Warrior

Iridescent Toad Publishing

Iridescent Toad Publishing.

Cover designed by RuthAndJohn.com/Creatives

First edition. ISBN: 978-1-9163478-8-5

Every day
That you spend on this earth
Is time
That you have to live
In your own head

You're there
No matter what

You owe it to yourself
To make it a good one

Define fight
Define battle
Is there one there?
And is it yours to be had?

You are the product
Of every experience
You've ever had
Good or bad
It has equipped you with knowledge

You've overcome
Every obstacle
So far
There's every hope
Every reason
That you will do so again

Be your own best friend

When you love yourself
It helps you to be kind

Kind to you
And kind to others

Of course there is
A lot of pain in the world
Break the chain
Be the difference
Wherever possible

The rain falls
In abundance
But it's preparing
Fertile ground
For life
With nourishment
With care

Rhythmic
Pulsing
Battle drums

Driving you on
Relentless
Tribal

Passion is good
It's a burning fire
Deep within you
Keep it alight
That's yours
For life
Never let it go out

Each new day
Is a new opportunity
We don't know
What's round the corner
But whatever it is
Believe that we're ready

Human traffic
Everyone fighting
Their own personal battle
So much love
For all the people

Every flower
That grows
Has been on a journey

From the potential of being
A tiny seed
Making the best
Of its surroundings
To become what it can

When a mouse
Gathers supplies
For the winter
They invest in their future
And they snuggle up
Safely
Prepared for the cold

You are the centre
Of your own enlightenment

Getting closer
To where you want to be
Every day
Just a little bit further
It all adds up

You only owe it to yourself
That's not selfish
That's love

It's harder to love others
By being a martyr

Your strength comes first

The ocean keeps moving
No matter what

You must too

Even when resting
You're still moving

Spiritually, you don't stand still

You are your home
You don't need someone else
To create that space

It's a big world out there
And you've only seen
A small fraction of it

And that's ok

Because it means
There's always more

Wherever possible
Expand your scope
Challenge yourself
Of course
Set realistic goals
But certainly
Keep building
Keep growing
See what happens
You've nothing to lose

Since the beginning of humanity
There has always been
Something to fear
Something to fight
Don't seek it
But don't hide

Set your own parameters
Your own values
Your own boundaries

If you meet your own approval
The thoughts of others
Won't matter

If you like yourself
You're already ahead of the game

Nobody knows
What "the game" actually is

But yeah

There are lots of signposts
In life
Designed
To make you
Feel bad

Boycott that
Feel free
Feel the wind in your hair
No special shampoo required

A day spent feeling
Is a day spent well

A day spent creating
Is a day spent well

No need to move mountains
To be the best you

Even trees go through phases
Yep, even the evergreen ones

They go through phases
Not by blossoming and shedding
But in how they weather everything
Wind, rain and sun

What tools can you use
To fight this beast?
What is it you feel?
Unarmed?
Unprepared?

Don't run mindlessly
Towards the beast
Bide your time
Strategise

Tomorrow
All your dreams
Could come true

Head in the clouds?
Well, perhaps

Doesn't matter

It doesn't need to be
Immediate
You've more to do
And that's ok

All journeys have peaks
All journeys have troughs
Even the most linear
Comes with dimensions

Every unique cloud
Is only formed once
Beautiful

The very fact
That you've been born
Makes you worthwhile
A masterpiece
A success

Welcome to the world
It's your right to be here

Every note
On the page
Gives beauty
To the music

Every tiny little note

The power of a hug
Deeply human

The power of alone time
No less fulfilling

Dance
Even when you can't move
Dance

Physical limits
Aren't spiritual limits

Practical limits
Aren't philosophical limits

When sunbeams come through the window
That's brightness

Stunning, inspiring, wonderful, brightness

Even on the darkest day

You attract the energy
That you give out

If you want good people
Make them feel welcome

The waxy resilience
Of a glossy red cherry
The pliable fruit inside
Protected and safe

Duvet days
Recuperation
Not defeat

In a world of many
Someone out there
Gets you
Understands you
Loves you

You may have yet to meet them
But they are out there

Some people
Like to tell you
There's a troll
Under the bridge

How would they know?
They lived to tell the tale

Lies or truth
If the bridge has your attention
Then maybe crossing it
Is the right choice for you

Besides
The troll might be friendly
Or at least
Not an enemy

Different fish
Different shapes
All looking good
In the sea

Be different
Not a problem

Many tangents
Where will they take you?

If you don't explore
You could miss out

You've got this

Even if you're filled
With dread
With reluctance
With fear
With doubt

You've got this

Because you have

There's no other way
And it's really that simple

When it comes to your mind
You're the leader

Nobody else has the right to your mind

That's yours

Nobody is born
An expert
At anything

That's why
Learning
Is liberating

Don't hate
What you don't know

Love
What you've yet to learn

You're already there
You're already you

Change is inevitable
Enjoy the ride

You're worthy
Of love
Of kindness
Of friendship

If anyone says you're not
Then please
Run away
If not physically
Then mentally

You can't control
What goes on
In the world

But you can control
How you perceive
How you process

You are so much more
Than the sum
Of mere opinions

You walk
You move
You travel through strife

The land is yours
Where will you go?

Every moment
Pleasant or hard
Is a moment lived

Pain
Or sorrow
Love and forgive

Who walks alongside us
Nobody knows

Feel it or not
The vibrancy glows

A rock
Strong and firm
Stubborn on the ground
The wind rushes past it
Never through it
Never moves it

Today
You are that rock

When someone extends
A branch of support
They give something
Of themselves

Love them
Thank them

A lifelong friend
Or a fleeting companion
What matters right now
Is today

They reached out
That's precious

Falling from a great height
Catch yourself
In a warming glow
A ball of light
Soft
Kind
Illuminated
Cocooned
Safe and ready
For the next round

Home now
Familiar sounds
Familiar smells
Closing the door
On the hectic outside

Silent and calm
Armour removed
You don't have to wear it
All of the time

Many options
Many guides
Take your pick
And be your own

So much choice
And critics too
It doesn't hurt
To walk alone

And just when you think
You've found your peak
The highest point
You'll ever go

Through those you meet
And how you grow
You might just learn
From what they show

Every little pebble makes a beach
Some get washed out to sea
Others sit dormant on the sand

Every little thought in your mind
Some to be cast away
Some to keep and be embraced

The salmon swimming
Up the stream
Pushed back
By the water's power

But every so often
Moments of glory
Overcoming a force
Stronger than itself

The strength of the wind
And yet the birds fly
Soaring, gliding
Free, yet aware

Born flightless
Potential always there
And when it's nurtured
They'll grace the air

A gentle source
Of reassuring comfort
Sleep can soothe

Hope and optimism
Can be frail
Please feed them
Please don't shove them away

Be realistic
But please don't forget
To plant those seeds
For good energy

Grey days happen
It would be weird
If they didn't

To pine for perfection
To a vast extent
Makes more days grey

If all we do
Is love
Wholeheartedly
Then that's a life
Lived well

Showered and dressed
Ready for the day
Mask applied
Armour refined
Out of the door
And not afraid

Every heartbeat
Gets you through
Each single one
Counts for something

Nobody needs
To walk a mile in your shoes
To care for you
And what you've been through

Anyone capable
With sound empathy
Will know there's a battle
We're all going through

A compass shows directions
That have been assigned names
North, North East, East
And so on

But for every direction with a name
There are so many
That exist unnamed
Maybe one of those will be yours

Swords, venom, bile
Whatever form it takes
We've all got a weapon

It's there if needed
But weaponry unused
Celebrates restraint

All the stars
How they align

Beautiful

Whose design
Nobody knows

But it all makes sense
Somehow

To rise from the ashes
Is so damn natural
Be that phoenix
Because you can

Surrounded by flames
And remnants charred
The creature emerges
Strong despite scars

Wind echoing
Of stories past
Whirling
Spiralling
Gliding fast

Carrying feeling
Made to last
Living
Breathing
Your story cast

The stability of the moon
And the howling wolf
Nature in cycle
At one with the earth

The butterfly
Spreading his wings
Showing his colours
Sharing his beauty

Coasting
On the wave of the breeze
Floating
A rainbow in motion

Dust in your eyes
From a sandstorm
Abrasive
Keep blinking

Blinking away
The grit
The dirt
The uncertainty

In search of clarity
Beautiful
Transparent
Certain clarity

Eating for nutrition
Feeding the body
All it needs
To be the best it can be

Training the mind
Nurturing thought
Informed thought
Independent thought

A safe and rational paradise
No matter what's outside

Ready for action
Not afraid
Calmly awaiting
What's next

Not on the edge
But alert enough
To take what comes
With a sense of flow

So many things
Come in stages
And in phases

Nothing stays still
And that's ok

Ignoring people
Who speak cruel words
Takes something away
From them:

Your attention

Their words rendered powerless

A sharp sword
Gets to the point
Cuts through
Objectively, it gets things done

A blunt sword
Has to work
Harder
You knew this; come prepared

A short silence
Can carry
Far more meaning
Than a barrage of noise

Speak carefully
Allow your words
To have impact
When they come

Listen selectively
Through all the noise
Only so much
Matters

There's no such thing
As a failure
They're all
Worthwhile experiments
On the path to success

Every so-called failure
Could be part
Of the process
That ultimately
Gets you there

You can't calm a storm
It will do what it does
Your thoughts can't stop it

The storm could work
In the cruellest of ways
Short and sharp, or long and brutal

While the storm rages on
Calm yourself
And sit tight
It soon will pass

Imagine if
You didn't pick
Your battles

Charging
At every problem
With full attack

You'd be drained
From constant war

You've only got
So much energy

So please
Pick your battles

Self-defence
More than a class
Lifelong knowledge

Thinking
Feeling
Living
Breathing
Beautiful
Human being

You

Lightning Source UK Ltd.
Milton Keynes UK
UKHW051121260123
415993UK00011B/101

9 781916 347885